God Bless Potatoes:

The Modernized Book of Potato Cookery

BY MRS. MARY L. WADE

first published 1918

Modernized and reprinted by
New York History Review, 2019

"*God Bless Potatoes: The Modernized Book of Potato Cookery*"
by Mrs. Mary L. Wade

originally published as *The Book of Potato Cookery* in 1918

Modernized and reprinted by New York History Review in 2019
Copyright ©2019 New York History Review. Some rights reserved.

ISBN-13: 978-1-950822-01-0

First Edition

Printed in the United States of America

Cover image: potatoes

Dedicated to those women patriots who are helping win the war, not with blare of trumpets, or in the light of publicity, but in their own homes, where by careful planning, and with much sacrifice of time and strength, they are giving their families varied and nourishing food, and at the same time are conserving the precious foodstuffs for our soldiers and allies "over there."

If this book proves a help to such women, the author has accomplished her purpose.

CONTENTS

CHAPTERS

I The Potato: Its Story and Importance............9

II Potatoes: Boiled, Mashed, Baked, Fried, etc..15

III Biscuits, Muffins, etc...............................39

IV Sweet Potatoes..47

V Potatoes with Meat and Fish....................51

VI Soups and Chowders..............................61

VII Salads..67

VIII Puddings and Cakes............................73

INDEX...83

God Bless Potatoes: Potato Cookery

THE POTATO: ITS STORY AND IMPORTANCE

CHAPTER I

THE POTATO: ITS STORY AND IMPORTANCE

There is no plant grown (excepting wheat) so important as the potato in the dietary of the nations at war. The potato so far surpasses all other tubers and roots in importance that its composition and nutritive value have been carefully studied both in this country and in Europe. It is a native of the elevated tropical valleys of Chile, Peru, and Mexico; and was carried to Spain from Peru early in the sixteenth century, introduced into Virginia from Florida by Spanish explorers, and into Great Britain from Virginia by Sir John Hawkins in 1565. Since that time, it has become a staple article of food throughout all Europe and the Americas, so commonly and universally used that it is to be found on the tables of rich and poor alike.

The potato is noteworthy for its extraordinary productiveness, far exceeding that of almost any other food product grown, an equal amount of ground yielding approximately thirty times greater weight of potatoes than of wheat. It is grown in all parts of the United States, but most abundantly in the North Atlantic and North Central States. New York, Maine, Michigan, and Wisconsin are the greatest potato states, each producing annually more than twenty million bushels.

FOOD VALUE

The bulk of the carbohydrates which the potato stores for future use is in the form of starch which, of course, is insoluble in cold water, and small quantities of dextrin sugar, etc., which are soluble. In young tubers there is a larger proportion of sugar and less starch than when they become mature. When it be- gins to sprout part of the starch is converted by a ferment into soluble glucose Fat appears in such small amounts that it need not be taken into account. The protein bodies are rather scant. The most important mineral matters found in potatoes are potash and phosphoric acid compounds. As ordinarily purchased 4.5 pounds of raw potatoes and 1 pound of uncooked rice contain equal weights of each class of nutrients and have about the same nutritive value.

In the ordinary American dietary, potatoes represent 3.9 per cent of the total cost of food, and furnish 5.3 per cent of the total calories, 4.2 per cent of the total protein, and 8.7 per cent of the total phosphorous and iron compounds. As phosphorous and iron compounds are of as much importance in the dietary as protein and fuel foods, it is evident that a generous supply of nutrients is obtained for a small percentage of money expended for potatoes.

Although the percentage of ash constituents in foods is small, the part they play in constructing tissue and in keeping the body in good working order is not a small one.

Phosphorous is essential in building tissue and in stimulating growth; iron is necessary in the making of red blood cells and other tissues. Calcium is needed in building bones and teeth. Vegetables furnish iron in larger proportions than do most animal foods. In the mineral content of potatoes are moderate amounts of the necessary compounds of phosphorous and calcium, a relatively high percentage of iron and a very high percentage of the base yielding potassium.

It is estimated that there are enough basic compounds in one medium-sized potato to neutralize the acids of two average slices of roast beef. If rice should be substituted in such a meal for potatoes, while the rice would supply the necessary starch, it would not serve to counteract the acids produced by the meat but would rather increase them.

"Vitamin" is the name given to a property or constituent of food which is essential to life — and potatoes possess this property. In the refining process wheat loses this vitamin property or constituent; therefore, the potato is especially beneficial in a dietary in which white bread is used.

MARKS OF THE GOOD POTATO

In point of flavor the early varieties and young potatoes generally are preferable to more mature ones. They usually have smoother skins than older ones. They are not as mealy and they do not keep as well. Late in the season well-developed tubers are safer. Very large ones are not desirable because it is harder to cook them evenly. Smooth, regularly shaped potatoes with comparatively few eyes are more economical than irregular ones which cannot be pared without much waste. Tubers old enough to sprout begin to develop an acrid taste. Watery potatoes are always undesirable because they become soggy in cooking. A good, mealy potato should feel firm when pressed in the hand. If cut it should separate crisply under the knife and be of even density throughout. When potatoes are old and wrinkled they are much improved by cutting off the ends or by paring and soaking in cold water for several hours.

SUGGESTIONS FOR THE PREPARATION AND COOKING OF POTATOES

The proper preparation of potatoes should never be considered of secondary importance, even if regarded from a purely hygienic standpoint only. The first essential to be observed in order to achieve the best results is scrupulous cleanliness. Special care should be given potatoes when cooked in their "jackets." They should be thoroughly scrubbed with a small brush and then rinsed.

Baking and steaming are generally thought to be the best ways of cooking potatoes; the latter method has the advantage of the economy of fuel, as a potato baked in a slow oven is inferior to one properly boiled. The method by which they are cooked should be considered not only for its effect on the nutrition, but upon the pocketbook.

When potatoes are pared before cooking, the loss is estimated at about twenty per cent, as the larger proportion of the protein and mineral matter is in the outer layer, and the skin tends to hold back the protein, mineral salts and starch. If the skin is removed before cooking the waste of total substance is about twice as much as when cooked in their skins. It is wasteful to pare potatoes long before cooking as they must be covered with cold water in order to keep them from turning dark. Potatoes pared and soaked three or four hours lose about three times as much of their mineral matter and seven times as much of their protein as those that are pared and put on to cook immediately. Therefore, the conclusion is that it is better not to pare potatoes before cooking, and to put them on to cook in boiling water so as to retain all their nutritive value. As potatoes are not always perfect, the housewife must use discretion as to the advisability of removing part, or all of the skin before cooking.

For frying in deep fat, or for salads, a potato high in protein and low in starch content is desirable; but for baking, mashing, and such purposes, a mealy potato is preferable.

CHAPTER II

POTATOES: BOILED, MASHED, BAKED, FRIED, ETC.

BOILED POTATOES

Select potatoes as nearly the same size as possible. If they are to be cooked in their skins scrub them and cut a narrow band of skin from each potato. If they are to be pared, remove as little as possible of the skin with a sharp knife and with the point of the knife remove the eyes and any imperfections. Cover with boiling water. Boil for fifteen minutes and add one tablespoon salt for every dozen potatoes. When they can be easily pierced with a fork they are done, which will be from twenty to thirty-five minutes according to size. Drain off every drop of water. If not to be served immediately cover with a clean cloth, but never with a tight cover.

MASHED POTATOES

When boiled potatoes are drained, remove skins, mash with wire potato masher until free from lumps. Add tablespoon butter for every four potatoes and enough hot milk to moisten. No definite amount of milk can be given as potatoes vary as to the amount they will absorb. Beat light and serve piled lightly in a hot dish.

Baked Potatoes

Select potatoes of even size with smooth surface. Scrub clean. Put into a hot oven and bake until soft, about forty to forty-five minutes. Test to see if they are soft by squeezing in a clean holder. If the skin breaks easily and they feel soft to the hand they are done. Each skin should be broken to allow the steam to escape. They should be served at once.

Potato Sauté

Wash, pare, and cut four potatoes in quarter-inch slices. Let stand in cold water one-half hour. Drain. Put two tablespoons of oil in frying pan. When hot put in potatoes. Cover closely. Set where they will cook slowly, and cook fifteen to twenty minutes. Stir occasionally.

Potatoes a la Maitre d'Hotel

Cut raw potatoes into cubes or balls with a French cutter and boil ten to fifteen minutes in salted water. Drain. Cream three tablespoons butter, add one teaspoon lemon juice, one-half teaspoon salt, one-eighth teaspoon paprika, two teaspoons chopped parsley. Add this to the potatoes and serve.

French Fried Potatoes

Wash and pare the potatoes. If small cut them in eighths lengthwise; or if large cut in half crosswise, then cut in pieces a quarter of an inch lengthwise. Soak for one hour in cold water. Drain and wipe dry. Fry a few at a time in hot fat until brown. Drain on soft paper and sprinkle with salt.

Hashed Brown Potatoes

Two cups cold boiled or baked potatoes chopped fine. Season with salt and pepper. Put two tablespoons fat in a frying pan. When hot add the potato and press down carefully into the bottom of the pan. Cook slowly until potatoes are brown on the bottom. Roll over carefully and turn on to a hot platter. Garnish with watercress and rings of pimento.

Baked Hashed Brown Potatoes

2 large potatoes
1 tablespoon chopped onion
1 tablespoon butter or favorite substitute
1 tablespoon minced parsley
1 tablespoon flour
1 cup milk or favorite substitute
1 teaspoon salt
1/4 teaspoon pepper

Wash and pare the potatoes and cut into dice. Melt the butter; blend with it the flour, salt, and pepper. Add the milk and stir until it boils. Butter a baking dish. Put in a layer of potato. Sprinkle over it half of the onion and parsley, then the remainder of the potato and onion and parsley. Pour the sauce over it and bake in a hot oven for half an hour, or until soft. Cover for the first fifteen minutes, then remove cover and brown.

POTATOES HASHED IN CREAM

Two cups cold cooked potatoes, hashed. Season with salt and pepper. Put into a saucepan with one cup thin cream. Place where it will heat but not brown. Cook until cream is all absorbed. Add one teaspoon butter. Shake occasionally while cooking.

POTATO PUFFS

1 cup cold boiled potato
1/2 cup cheese
1/2 cup barley flour
1/2 cup butter or favorite substitute
2 eggs
1/2 teaspoon salt
1/8 teaspoon cayenne

Either grate or rub through a strainer the potato (one cupful after grating) and the cheese. Melt the butter and when it is bubbling stir the flour in quickly and stir over the fire until it cleaves from the side of the pan. Remove from the fire. Cool slightly. Add the unbeaten eggs one at a time, beating thoroughly after each egg is added. Add cheese, potato, salt and cayenne, and again beat.

Drop by spoonfuls on a well buttered pan and bake for half an hour in a moderately hot oven.

Potato Soufflé

2 cups hot mashed potato
1/2 cup milk
1 tablespoon butter or favorite substitute
1/2 teaspoon salt
1/4 teaspoon pepper
2 eggs

To the mashed potato add all the ingredients except the whites of eggs, and beat until light. Cool. Beat the whites stiff and dry and fold lightly into the potato. Put into a buttered baking dish and bake until puffed up and brown. Serve at once in the dish in which it is baked. If liked more delicate, omit the yolks.

Curried Potatoes

6 cold cooked potatoes (boiled or baked)
1 teaspoon salt
1/4 teaspoon pepper
2 tablespoons butter or favorite substitute
1 scant teaspoon curry powder
1/2 cup stock or milk or favorite substitute
1 tablespoon chopped onion
1 tablespoon lemon juice

Melt the butter. Add onion. Cook two or three minutes, but do not brown. Add potatoes, salt, pepper and curry powder and mix well with the onion. Add the stock or milk and lemon juice. Stir gently with a fork until all the liquid is absorbed. Serve sprinkled with chopped parsley.

Potato Scallop

1 cup cold boiled potato - diced
2 tablespoons chopped celery
1 tablespoon chopped onion
2 tablespoons chopped carrot (add any cooked peas or string beans which you may have on hand)
1 cup strained tomato
2 tablespoons butter or favorite substitute
1 tablespoon flour
sifted bread crumbs

Melt the butter. Cook in it the onion, carrot, and celery for two or three minutes. Add the flour. Stir until blended. Add the tomato; stir until it boils. Grease a baking dish. Sprinkle over with the crumbs. Put in the potatoes and other vegetables. Pour the sauce over it. Cover with buttered crumbs and bake until brown.

Potato Fricassee

1 cup cold boiled or baked potato - diced
½ teaspoon onion juice
1 cup milk or favorite substitute
1 tablespoon butter or favorite substitute
1 tablespoon cream
1/2 teaspoon salt
2 egg yolks or favorite substitute
1/4 teaspoon pepper

Melt the butter. Add the milk, potato and seasonings. Heat slowly. Beat the egg yolks and cream together. Stir into the potato.

When thickened remove from the fire at once and pour into a hot serving dish. Sprinkle with chopped parsley and serve at once.

POTATOES WITH CHIVES

4 medium potatoes
2 tablespoons butter or favorite substitute
1/4 cup hot milk or favorite substitute
2 tablespoons chopped chives

Wash, pare and boil potatoes. Mash them. Add the other ingredients: beat until light. Turn into a buttered baking dish; leave the top rough. Dot over with pieces of butter and bake until golden brown in a hot oven.

POTATO HILLOCKS

2 cups hot mashed potato
2 tablespoons melted butter or favorite substitute
2 tablespoons hot milk or favorite substitute
1 egg or favorite substitute
1/2 teaspoon salt
a few grains of pepper

Add butter, milk, salt, pepper and beaten egg to the potato. Shape into pyramids. Place on a greased pan. Baste with the butter. Brown in a hot oven. Slip off carefully onto a hot platter. These may be served as a garnish around meat or by themselves with cheese sauce. If served with cheese sauce it may be used as the main dish at dinner or luncheon.

Potato Omelette

1 medium baked potato
1/2 teaspoon salt
1/4 teaspoon lemon juice
1/2 tablespoon butter or favorite substitute
3 eggs or favorite substitute
1/4 teaspoon pepper

Peel the potato and rub through a fine strainer. Add the salt, pepper, and lemon juice. Separate the eggs and beat both whites and yolks until light. Add the yolks to the potato and beat well together. Fold the whites in lightly. Put butter in frying pan. When bubbling pour in the omelet. Cook slowly until brown, about eight or ten minutes. Turn onto a hot platter. An omelet is best cooked if placed in the oven for the last four or five minutes. If not put in the oven, slip an asbestos mat under the pan, reduce the heat, and cover the omelet that length of time.

Kalecanon or Colcannon

Chop fine equal quantities of cold cooked potato and cabbage. Season highly with salt, mustard and cayenne. Put some oil or fat (meat dripping is best) into a frying pan. When hot turn in the mixture; cook slowly without stirring until heated through.

Delmonico Potatoes

2 cups cold boiled potato, cut fine
2 tablespoons melted butter or favorite substitute
1 teaspoon salt
1/4 teaspoon pepper
1 cup rich milk or favorite substitute

Butter a shallow baking dish. Put in the seasoned potatoes. Pour over the milk and lastly the melted butter. Brown in a moderately hot oven. Serve in the dish in which they are cooked.

Potatoes and Onions
To serve with sausage

4 potatoes boiled in their skins (peel while hot and slice thin)
2 large onions (slice and let stand in salt water for 30 minutes)
(peel while hot and slice thin)

Melt one tablespoon of ham or bacon fat (or other fat will do). Add the onions and cook until slightly browned. Add the potato. Mix lightly with a fork. Add one-half cup vinegar, one-half teaspoon salt, and a few grains of cayenne, and cook five minutes.

POTATO PIE

2 cups sliced raw potato
1 onion, sliced
1 stalk celery, sliced
2 tablespoons butter or favorite substitute
2 tablespoons tapioca
1/2 cup milk or favorite substitute
1/2 teaspoon salt
1/2 cup water

Melt the butter and cook the onion in it, but do not brown. Add the water. Butter a pudding dish and put in it the potatoes, celery, salt, onion, and water. Sprinkle the tapioca over. Add the milk and cover with the following paste:

1 cup hot mashed potato
4 tablespoons of shortening
2 teaspoons baking powder enough milk to make a soft dough
1/2 teaspoon salt
1 cup corn flour

Bake one hour in a moderate oven.

FRANCONIA POTATOES (BAKED WITH MEAT)

Wash and pare the potatoes and cut into uniform size (about one and a half inch cubes). Parboil five minutes. Drain. Put into the roasting pan with the meat and baste often with the fat from the meat. Cook forty minutes.

Potato Chops

4 medium potatoes or enough to make 2 cups
2 tablespoons green pepper
2 tablespoons carrot
1 cup hot milk or favorite substitute
1/2 tablespoon onion
3 tablespoons tomato pulp
1 egg yolk or favorite substitute
3 tablespoons sifted crumbs
2 tablespoons sherry, or Madeira wine
3 tablespoons butter or favorite substitute
1/4 teaspoon mace
1 teaspoon salt
1 teaspoon parsley
cayenne

Wash, pare, and chop the potatoes fine, and cook in the milk until soft (use care that they do not burn). When soft add the butter. Put the pepper, carrot, onion, and parsley through the food chopper and stir into the potato. Cook a few moments stirring constantly. Add the tomato pulp, salt, cayenne, mace, and wine. Cool. Form into chops. Roll in egg and crumbs. Fry in deep fat, or roll in flour and melted fat and brown in a hot oven.

Make the tomato pulp by cooking strained tomato until thick. If the wine is objectionable use a tablespoon of lemon juice in its place.

POTATO BOUCHÉES

1 cup hot mashed potato
2 tablespoons hot milk or favorite substitute
1 beaten yolk of egg or favorite substitute
1 tablespoon butter or favorite substitute
3 tablespoons cheese - shredded
onion salt
salt and pepper
a few grains of cayenne
cabbage leaves

Mix all the ingredients together. Season to taste and beat until light. Wash and drain tender cabbage leaves or the large outside leaves of lettuce. Put one spoonful of the potato mixture in each leaf; wrap the leaf around it, and fasten with a wooden toothpick. Steam for twenty minutes. Remove the toothpick and serve. The above will make eight or nine bouchees.

Potatoes with Peanut Butter

2 cups cold boiled or baked potato
1/2 tablespoon butter or favorite substitute
1/2 teaspoon salt
1/4 teaspoon pepper
2 tablespoons peanut butter
yolks of 2 hardboiled eggs
milk or favorite substitute

Cut potatoes into dice. Melt butter in saucepan. Put the potatoes in. Season with salt and pepper. Add the milk, and simmer until most of the milk is absorbed. Blend the peanut butter and yolks of eggs together and stir into the potato. Serve when hot.

Potato Balls

Grate three or four cold boiled potatoes. Cream one-third cup butter and work into it three beaten eggs. Blend this with the potato. Add salt and pepper. Shape into small balls. Drop into boiling water with a little salt in it. Simmer for ten minutes. Serve with meat gravy or tomato sauce.

Tomato Sauce

1 1/2 cups strained tomato
1/2 tablespoon onion juice
2 tablespoons oil
1 1/2 tablespoons cornstarch
1/2 teaspoon salt
1/4 teaspoon pepper

Heat oil in pan. Blend with it the cornstarch and seasonings. Pour in the tomato and stir until it thickens. Simmer for ten minutes.

Potato Cakes

6 medium potatoes
2 tablespoons butter
1 teaspoon minced onion
3 tablespoons milk or favorite substitute
¼ teaspoon mace
cayenne
2 egg yolks or favorite substitute
3 tablespoons fine bread crumbs
1/2 teaspoon salt

After removing skins from either boiled or baked potatoes, mash them through a fine strainer. Soak the crumbs for five or ten minutes in the milk. Add the soaked crumbs, salt, mace, and cayenne, and the yolks beaten light. Make into cakes. Dip into melted fat and place in a hot oven until brown. Serve with cheese sauce.

Cheese Sauce

1 tablespoon butter or favorite substitute
1 1/4 tablespoons flour
1/2 teaspoon salt
1/4 teaspoon paprika
1 cup cheese - shredded
1 cup milk or favorite substitute

Melt the butter. Add flour, salt, and paprika. When blended add the milk, and stir until it boils. Stir in the cheese and cook over water until the cheese is melted and smooth.

POTATO NESTS WITH CHEESE

4 medium potatoes
1 tablespoon butter or favorite substitute
1/2 teaspoon salt
2 tablespoons grated cheese
a few grains of paprika
2 tablespoons thin cream
2 egg yolks or favorite substitute

Boil and mash the potatoes. Add the butter, cheese and seasonings. Beat the egg yolks with the cream and mix with the potato. Make into nests, and place on a greased baking tin. Brush over with the beaten white of egg and set in the oven to brown. Slip carefully off onto a hot platter and fill the centers with hot seasoned peas.
Potato nests are also good filled with creamed chicken or fish.

POTATO CHEESE SOUFFLÉ

2 medium potatoes
3 tablespoons grated cheese
1 tablespoon butter or favorite substitute
1 cup milk or favorite substitute
1 tablespoon cream
1 egg

Boil the potatoes in their jackets. When soft remove skins and set away to cool. When cold, grate or rub through wire strainer. Add the cheese, butter and milk. Beat the egg yolk with the cream and add to potato. Beat white of egg light and dry and fold in lightly. Pour into a buttered mold and bake one-half hour, or steam one hour, tightly covered. Serve at once.

Potato Gruyére

Allow one potato for each person. Scrub and bake. When done open and scrape the inside into a hot bowl. Mash. For each potato add one teaspoon butter, two teaspoons grated Gruyére cheese, salt and pepper to taste, and the stiffly beaten white of one egg for every three potatoes. Form into heaps on a buttered pan. Brush over with beaten yolk of egg diluted with a little milk. Brown in a hot oven.

Potatoes with Cheese Stuffing

3 large potatoes
2 whites of eggs or favorite substitute
3 tablespoons grated cheese
1 yolk of egg
2 tablespoons milk or favorite substitute
2 tablespoons butter or margarine
1/2 teaspoon salt
1 teaspoon chopped parsley
1/4 teaspoon pepper

Bake the potatoes. When done cut in halves lengthwise. Remove the insides to a hot bowl and add to them the cheese, milk, butter, salt, pepper, and yolk of egg. Beat the whites of eggs stiff and fold in lightly. Fill the skins with the mixture, heaping it up. Leave the tops rough. Brush them over with yolk of egg diluted with one tablespoon milk. Bake in oven until brown.

Potato Roll

4 medium potatoes
1/2 teaspoon salt
yolks of 3 eggs
1/4 cup cream
1 teaspoon finely minced onion
2 tablespoons butter or favorite substitute

Wash, pare, and boil the potatoes and rub through sieve. Beat the yolks with the cream and mix with the potato. Add the butter and seasonings. Butter a mold and sprinkle with bread crumbs. Put in the mixture. Set mold in a pan of hot water. Cover with oiled paper and bake for fifteen minutes. Remove the paper and bake for fifteen minutes longer. Serve with Hollandaise Sauce.

Hollandaise Sauce

1/2 cup butter or favorite substitute
1/4 teaspoon salt
yolks of 2 eggs
a few grains cayenne
juice of 1/2 lemon
1/2 cup boiling water

Cream the butter. Add one egg yolk and beat it well into the butter, then the second egg yolk, and when well mixed add the salt, cayenne, and boiling water. Cook over boiling water, stirring constantly about two minutes until like thick cream. Remove from the fire at once and turn into dish to serve.

Philadelphia Potatoes

new potatoes, enough to make 3 cups
1 egg
1 tablespoon cream
2 tablespoons butter or favorite substitute
2 teaspoons cornstarch
1/2 teaspoon salt
1/2 cup milk or favorite substitute
1/4 teaspoon pepper

Boil the potatoes and remove the skins. Cut in thin slices. Make a sauce with the butter, cornstarch, and milk. Season with salt and pepper. Butter a shallow dish. Put in half the potato; add half the sauce, then repeat. Beat the egg with the cream and pour over the last thing. Bake in a hot oven until egg is set.

Kentucky Potatoes

5 medium potatoes
2 tablespoons butter or favorite substitute
1/3 teaspoon white pepper
1 1/2 cups milk or favorite substitute
3/4 teaspoon salt

Wash, pare, and slice the potatoes. Soak in cold water one-half hour. Drain and put into a greased baking dish. Season with salt and pepper. Pour over the milk and put the butter in bits over the top. Bake in a hot oven, about forty-five minutes until soft. Cover for the first twenty minutes.

Norwegian Potatoes

2 cups raw potato cut - diced
½ cup chopped raw onion
2 tablespoons butter or favorite substitute
1 cup chopped raw carrot
1 teaspoon salt
1/4 teaspoon pepper

Melt the butter. Cook in it the onion and carrot (but do not brown them), for five minutes. Add the potato, salt, and pepper. Add enough boiling water to cover. Cover and simmer for half an hour. Watch carefully that the water does not boil away and the vegetables burn. Remove the cover and cook until most of the water has evaporated.

SCOTCH POTATOES

2 cups potato
1 1/2 tablespoons cornstarch or rice flour
1 1/2 cups onion
1 cup milk or favorite substitute
1 1/2 teaspoons salt
1 tablespoon butter or favorite substitute
1/8 teaspoon pepper

Wash, pare, and cut potato and onion in quarter-inch slices. Cover with boiling water. Add one teaspoon salt and cook ten minutes. Drain. Put into a greased baking dish. Make a sauce by melting the butter; blend with it the cornstarch or rice flour, one-half teaspoon salt, and pepper. Add the milk and stir until it thickens. Pour this over the potatoes and onion. Put small pieces of butter over the top and bake thirty to forty minutes.

SWISS POTATOES

Cut four cold boiled potatoes into thin slices. Break into small pieces half as much cheese as there is potato. Put alternate layers of potatoes and cheese into a well-buttered baking dish with a layer of potatoes on top. Pour one-fourth cup milk over all and dot the top with pieces of butter. Bake in a moderate oven until light brown.

FRENCH POTATOES

Cut cold boiled potatoes into slices one-fourth inch thick. Sauté in a little butter or margarine. Keep slices whole if possible. When brown on both sides add more butter and a little chopped parsley, salt, pepper, and lemon juice. When hot add a little hot cream, and serve.

CHILIAN POTATOES

Mashed potatoes seasoned with salt, butter, Tabasco, and milk. Press into a loaf pan. Chill. When cold cut into half-inch slices. Roll in flour. Sauté in oil.

POTATOES MEXICAN STYLE

5 medium potatoes
1/2 tablespoon parsley
1/4 cup seeded raisins
1 teaspoon sugar
10 olives stuffed with pimento
1/2 teaspoon salt
cayenne

After scrubbing, paring, and boiling the potatoes rub hem through a fine strainer. Put raisins, olives, and parsley through the meat chopper and add the potato. Add sugar, salt, and a few grains of cayenne. Form into an oblong cake and leave the top rough. Put two teaspoons of margarine or vegetable oil into a baking tin and heat. Put in the cake and bake for fifteen minutes or until a golden brown. Take out carefully onto a hot platter and serve.

POTATO AND SPINACH CROQUETTES

2 cups hot mashed potato
2 tablespoons butter
2 eggs - beaten
1/2 cup cooked spinach chopped fine
1/2 teaspoon salt
1/4 teaspoon pepper
bread crumbs

Mix all the ingredients together. Cool. Shape into croquettes. Roll in egg and crumbs and fry in deep fat, or roll in flour and dip in melted fat and cook in a hot oven until brown.

POTATO AND NUT CROQUETTES (1)

1 cup mashed potato
1/2 teaspoon salt
1 cup chopped nuts
1/4 teaspoon pepper
1 teaspoon onion juice
2 tablespoons milk or favorite substitute
1 teaspoon lemon juice
1 egg or favorite substitute

Mix potato, meat, onion juice, pepper, salt, and lemon juice together. Beat the egg and add the milk. Mix with the potato mixture. Shape, prepare, and cook as other croquettes.

POTATO AND NUT CROQUETTES (2)

1 cup mashed potato
1 cup soft bread crumbs
1/2 teaspoon salt
1/2 teaspoon lemon juice
1 cup chopped walnuts
2 eggs or favorite substitute- scrambled
1/2 teaspoon celery salt
3 tablespoons milk or favorite substitute

Mix all the ingredients together. Make into croquettes and fry.

CHAPTER III

BISCUITS, MUFFINS, ETC.

Raised Potato Biscuit

1 cup hot mashed potato
1 teaspoon salt
3 tablespoons shortening
1/2 cup milk or favorite substitute
1/2 yeast cake dissolved in 1/2 cup warm water
2 1/2 cups rice flour enough wheat flour to knead
1 tablespoon sugar

Add the shortening, salt, sugar, and milk to the potato. When cool add the yeast and rice flour. Then add enough white flour to make stiff enough to knead. Knead well and set in a warm place to rise. When light and porous cut down with a knife. Shape into biscuit. Put into baking pan. Let rise again and bake for half an hour in a moderately hot oven. This is also good made into a loaf, and does not need as much shortening as when made into biscuit.

Potato Biscuit (1)

1 cup mashed potato
2 tablespoons shortening
1 cup corn flour
1 cup wheat flour
4 teaspoons baking powder
1 teaspoon salt
milk enough to make a soft dough

Sift together the flour, baking powder, and salt. Put in shortening with tips of fingers. Add the potato, and enough milk to make a soft dough. Turn onto a floured board. Roll to half-inch thickness, cut with biscuit cutter, and bake in a moderately hot oven for half an hour.

Potato Biscuit (2)

1 cup cold leftover mashed potatoes
1 tablespoon flour
1 tablespoon melted butter

Turn onto a floured board. Roll to inch thickness. Cut with biscuit cutter. Put onto a greased sheet one-half inch apart. Bake in a hot oven until brown. Split, butter, and serve while hot.

English Muffins

1 large potato
1 yeast cake dissolved in 1/2 cup water
1 teaspoon salt
1 1/2 cups boiling water

Wash and pare the potato and boil. When soft rub through a sieve. Add the water. When cool add the yeast. Beat well, and add two cups of rice flour and enough wheat flour to make a stiff dough. Cover and let rise until light and porous. Turn onto a board, dredged with flour. Divide in pieces. Roll in round shape. Let them set on board to rise again until full of bubbles. Have the griddle greased and warm. Slip the muffins on carefully. When cooked on one side turn and cook on the other. Do not have the griddle too hot, as they are liable to burn before being thoroughly cooked. When cold split and toast. These may be baked in the oven.

Potato and Corn Muffins

1 cup mashed potato
1 tablespoon oil
1 cup white corn meal
1 egg or favorite substitute
1 cup hot milk or favorite substitute
1/2 teaspoon salt
2 tablespoons sugar

Beat the potato, meal, and milk together. Add the fat, sugar, and yolk of egg beaten light. Beat until light and fold in the white of egg beaten stiff. Drop into greased muffin pans. Bake for thirty minutes in a moderately hot oven.

POTATO, RYE, AND OATMEAL MUFFINS

1 cup mashed potato
2 tablespoons corn syrup
1/2 cup fine ground oatmeal
1/2 cup milk or favorite substitute
1/2 cup rye flour
1 egg
1 teaspoon baking powder
1/2 teaspoon salt

Beat the egg light. Add the milk and syrup. Sift the salt, baking powder, and flour together, and add with the potato and oatmeal to the first mixture. Put into greased muffin pans and bake for one-half hour.

POTATO SCONES

1 cup mashed potato
3 teaspoons baking powder
1 1/2 cups barley flour
2 tablespoons oil
1 teaspoon salt
1 egg - beaten or favorite substitute
milk to moisten

Sift together flour, salt, and baking powder. Mix butter in lightly with tips of fingers. Add the potato, other ingredients, and the egg. Enough milk to moisten. Divide in two parts and roll each part one inch thick, keeping it round. Cut in quarters and bake in a hot oven or on a griddle. Turn when brown on one side. Serve hot.

Scotch Bannocks

1 cup mashed potato
1 cup fine oatmeal
1/2 teaspoon soda
1/2 teaspoon salt
1 tablespoon corn syrup
1 tablespoon melted butter or favorite substitute
buttermilk or favorite substitute

Mix together the potato, oatmeal, soda, salt, fat, and syrup. Add enough buttermilk to make into a soft dough. Form into balls with the hand and then flatten until half an inch thick. Cook on the griddle or in a moderately hot oven. When done split and spread with honey or syrup.

POTATO NOODLES

1 cup mashed potato
1 egg - beaten
1/2 cup wheat flour
1/2 teaspoon salt
rice flour
dash nutmeg

Add salt and slightly beaten egg to potatoes. Add the wheat flour and enough rice flour to knead into a stiff dough. Turn onto a floured board. You can make any kind of shape that you like. Rolled, formed, thick or thin. To be used in soups or cooked in rapidly boiling water until done to your taste, and served with meat or with cheese sauce. Or after boiling, pan fry until golden brown.

POTATO PANCAKES (1)

3 medium cold boiled potatoes
1 teaspoon baking powder
I small onion
2 eggs or favorite substitute
1/2 teaspoon salt
1 tablespoon oil
1/4 teaspoon pepper
enough barley flour to mix

Rub through a strainer or grate the potatoes. Mince the onion very fine. Beat the eggs light. Sift one-half cup barley flour with the baking powder. Mix altogether and add enough barley flour to make stiff enough to drop from spoon. Drop by spoonfuls on a hot greased griddle. When brown turn and brown on other side.

POTATO PANCAKES (2)

4 potatoes
2 eggs or favorite substitute
1 tablespoon fine bread crumbs
1/2 teaspoon salt

Pare and grate the potatoes. Separate the eggs. Add the yolks with the salt and bread crumbs to the potato. Beat whites of eggs stiff and fold in lightly. Drop by spoonfuls onto a greased griddle. When brown on one side turn and brown on other. Do not have the griddle too hot.

POTATO DUMPLINGS (1)

2 or 3 medium potatoes
¼ teaspoon salt
1/4 teaspoon mace
1 tablespoon sifted bread crumbs
1 teaspoon butter
1 egg or favorite substitute

Bake the potatoes. Scoop out insides and rub through a sieve. There should be one cupful. When cold add the other ingredients, and the egg well beaten. Flour the hands. Make into balls and drop into boiling salted water. Simmer for fifteen minutes.

Potato Dumplings (2)

1 large cold boiled potato
½ teaspoon salt
2 eggs or favorite substitute
1 teaspoon baking powder
corn flour

Grate the potato. Add salt and beaten eggs. Sift one-fourth cup corn flour with the baking powder. Stir into the potato mixture and add enough corn flour to form into balls. Roll into balls about one and one-half inches in diameter. Bake for half an hour or steam for three-quarters of an hour. Serve with meat or as a dessert with fruit sauce.

Potato Quenelles

2 cups hot mashed potato
1 tablespoon butter or favorite substitute
2 tablespoons cream or favorite substitute
1 teaspoon minced parsley
1/2 teaspoon salt
1/4 teaspoon pepper
2 eggs or favorite substitute
2 tablespoons minced ham

Add butter, parsley, salt, pepper, and ham to the potato. Add the yolk of eggs beaten with the cream. Add the whites beaten stiff. Shape into oval *quenelles* on a teaspoon with a spatula. Drop into smoking hot fat. Drain on soft paper.

SWEET POTATOES

CHAPTER IV

SWEET POTATOES

Considering both composition and digestibility it may be said that the nutritive value of sweet potatoes is much the same as that of white potatoes, and that they are well fitted to occupy the same place in the diet, and furnish a palatable substitute for white potatoes. In the North they usually cost more than white potatoes. In the South they are quite as cheap or cheaper than white potatoes.

BAKED SWEET POTATOES

Wash and bake the same as white potatoes. Small ones will bake in about one-half hour.

BOILED SWEET POTATOES

Wash but do not pare. Put into boiling water and cook fifteen to twenty minutes. Remove the skin and put into the oven for ten or fifteen minutes, or until soft. Potatoes are much sweeter and drier when cooked this way than when boiled until soft. Very large potatoes should be boiled longer.

Browned Sweet Potatoes

Prepare as above except split in halves after boiling and peeling. Put into a baking pan and baste with meat drippings. Season with salt. Cook in oven until soft, basting every ten minutes.

Glazed Sweet Potatoes

Cut cooked sweet potatoes into slices one-half inch thick. Spread butter or margarine over the bottom of baking dish. Cover with a layer of potatoes spread with corn syrup. Dot over with bits of butter. Add another layer of potato, corn syrup, and bits of butter. Pour one-fourth cup hot water over all. Bake for half an hour in a hot oven, or until the potatoes are glazed.

Fried Sweet Potatoes

Cut cold cooked potatoes into slices and fry brown in any clean fat.

Sweet Potatoes with Apples

Butter a baking dish. Put in a thick layer of cold cooked sweet potatoes cut in thin slices. Cover with apples which have been pared, cored and cut in thin slices. Pour one-third cup corn syrup over them. Dot over with bits of butter and sprinkle on a little salt. Bake thirty to forty minutes in a moderately hot oven, keeping the potatoes covered during the first fifteen minutes.

SWEET POTATOES WITH ORANGE

Cut cooked sweet potatoes into cubes. Butter a pudding dish. Put in a layer of potato and two tablespoons of corn syrup, and a little of the grated yellow rind of orange, a few grains of salt, and a little nutmeg. Dot over with bits of butter. Put in another layer of potato and add corn syrup, orange rind, salt, nutmeg, and butter, as before. Add juice of two oranges, one tablespoon lemon juice, and two tablespoons water Bake in moderate oven thirty to forty minutes.

SWEET POTATO CROQUETTES

2 cups hot mashed sweet potato
1/2 teaspoon salt
1/8 teaspoon pepper
3 tablespoons butter or favorite substitute
1 egg - beaten or favorite substitute

If not moist enough add a little hot milk. Shape and roll in flour, then in egg diluted with water, then in crumbs, and fry in deep fat. Drain on soft paper

POTATOES WITH MEAT AND FISH

CHAPTER V

POTATOES WITH MEAT AND FISH

A Complete Meal

6 potatoes
1 teaspoon salt
1 pound of the cheapest cut of lamb or mutton
1 onion
1 cup strained tomato
1/4 teaspoon pepper

Have a kettle with a close-fitting cover. Wash, pare, and slice the potatoes. Skin and slice the onion. Cut meat into small pieces. Put into the kettle alternate layers of the meat, potato, onion, and seasonings. Begin and finish with the potato. Pour over the strained tomato. Put on the cover and tie a dampened cloth closely over the top so no steam can escape. This can be cooked over water, or in a slow oven. Cook three or four hours. After removing from the fire let it stand five minutes before removing cloth and cover. In cooking this way none of the nutrients are lost.

Giblet Stew

Wash the giblets and neck and ends of wings. Cover with one quart water. Bring quickly to the boiling point. Simmer for one hour. Remove the meat from the neck and wings and chop with the giblets. Return to the kettle and add:

1 cup potato - diced
1 tablespoon chopped onion
5 fresh mushrooms - sliced

Simmer for twenty minutes. Add:

1 teaspoon salt
1 tablespoon chicken fat
1 tablespoon flour blended with 1 tablespoon chicken fat
1/4 teaspoon pepper

Stir into the stew and cook for five minutes. Take from the fire and add one tablespoon chopped parsley and the beaten yolks of two eggs.

Cottage Pie

Use any cold cooked meat, which may all of one kind or a mixture of several kinds. Season highly with chopped onion, salt, and pepper. Add chopped olives or chopped peppers if liked. Cover with mashed potato. Dot the top over with pieces of butter. Bake in a hot oven until well browned.

Pepper Pot

1 cup cold boiled potato
6 fresh mushrooms
1 cup cooked tripe cut in small pieces
1 cup cooked chicken - diced
1 tablespoon minced onion - diced
1 teaspoon salt
1 tablespoon minced parsley
2 tablespoons butter or favorite substitute
2 cups bouillon or stock
4 or 5 drops Tabasco sauce
1 tablespoon flour
1/4 teaspoon paprika
a few grains cayenne

Melt the butter. Add the onion, flour, and stock. When smooth add the other ingredients. Simmer for fifteen minutes and serve.

Savory Liver

1 pound calf's liver
1 cup water
2 small onions
2 cups potato
1 teaspoon salt
1/4 teaspoon sage
1/4 teaspoon pepper

Have the liver cut in slices, and pour boiling water over it. Drain and wipe dry. Cut in pieces about one-inch square. Slice the potatoes and onions. Grease a baking dish. Put in a layer of potatoes, then onion and liver and seasonings. Repeat until all is used. Pour on the water. Cover with greased paper and bake slowly one hour. Remove the paper the last quarter of an hour. Serve with apple or other tart fruit sauce.

Liver *en* Casserole

1 calf's liver
1/2 cup stock or water
1 1/2 cups fresh peas
2 cups potatoes - diced
1 cup carrots - diced
2 onions -minced
2 tablespoons butter or favorite substitute
4 fresh mushrooms
1 tablespoon flour

Cream the butter and flour and spread over the bottom of casserole. Cut the potato and carrot into dice and mince the onion. Put these with the peas and mushrooms in the casserole. Season with salt and pepper, and add the stock. Put the liver on top of these. Cover and bake in a moderately hot oven one hour. Serve in the casserole.

Potatoes and Sausage

Cut large smooth potatoes into halves lengthwise. Take out part of the center and fill the cavity with sausage meat. Tie halves together tightly with kitchen string. Put into a baking tin and bake in a hot oven until potatoes are soft.

BAKED HAM AND POTATOES

2 cups cold mashed potatoes
1 teaspoon prepared mustard
1 beaten egg or favorite substitute
1 cup milk or favorite substitute
1 cup chopped cooked ham
grated cheese of your choice

Mix together. Put into a greased baking dish. Sprinkle the top with grated cheese and bake twenty to thirty minutes.

POTATO CASSEROLE

One quart of hot mashed potato seasoned with milk, butter, and salt. Cool and add the beaten yolks of two eggs. Make into a wall on a fireproof serving dish. Brush over with white of egg and place in oven to brown. Cut any cold meat into small pieces and heat in the gravy, or for white meat make a white sauce and heat the meat in it. Fill the potato casserole with the prepared meat.

Potato Croustades

2 cups mashed potato
2 tablespoons butter or favorite substitute
2 tablespoons milk or favorite substitute
flour
2 egg yolks or favorite substitute
1/2 teaspoon salt
creamed meat or fish

To the mashed potato add butter, milk, salt, and beaten yolks of eggs. Turn on to a well-floured board and make into a roll three-inches thick. Cut off pieces one inch thick. Brush over with beaten white of egg. With a small cutter mark a lid. Bake in a hot oven until brown. Lift off the lid and scoop out part of the inside. Fill with creamed meat or fish.

Stuffing for Roast Goose or Duck (1)

2 cups mashed potato
1/2 teaspoon sage
1 cup sausage meat fried and broken into bits
1 cup fine bread crumbs
1 tablespoon minced onion
1 beaten egg or favorite substitute
1 teaspoon salt
a few grains cayenne

Mix together and use as stuffing.

Stuffing for Roast Goose (2)

Pare and boil four medium-sized potatoes and one onion until soft. Drain and mash. Add one-fourth cup milk, one tablespoon dried and crushed sage leaves, one and one-half teaspoons salt, one-half teaspoon pepper, and one cup soft bread crumbs.

Fish á la Murphy

Remove skin, head, and tail from a fish weighing four or five pounds. Lay one fillet on a greased fish sheet. Sprinkle with salt and brush over with lemon juice. Place on this a layer of mashed potato which has been well seasoned with salt, pepper, and onion juice and a liberal amount of butter. Cover the potato with the other fillet. Sprinkle with salt and lemon juice and brush over with melted butter. Bake thirty to forty minutes in a moderately hot oven. Serve with Hollandaise Sauce. Haddock, cod, whitefish, or any other light-colored fish may be cooked in this way.

Scalloped Herring

3 salt herrings
butter or favorite substitute
6 or 7 cold cooked potatoes
cayenne
2 cups of milk or favorite substitute
2 eggs or favorite substitute

Remove skin and bone from fish and cut into inch squares. Slice the potatoes. Beat the eggs slightly and add the milk. Butter a baking dish. Put in a layer of potato, then a layer of fish. Dot over with bits of butter and shake on a little cayenne. Then another layer of potato, and fish, butter, and cayenne, and lastly the potato. Pour over the milk and egg. Cover with buttered crumbs and bake thirty to forty minutes.

Fish and Potato Scallop

3 cups raw potato cut in cubes
1 1/2 cups salt cod fish cut in small pieces
1 tablespoon chopped onion
2 tablespoons butter or favorite substitute
2 tablespoons flour
1/2 teaspoon salt
1/4 teaspoon pepper
2 cups milk or favorite substitute
3/4 cup buttered bread crumbs

Cook the fish and potato together for ten minutes. Drain. Melt the butter; add onion and cook a few moments, but do not brown. Add the flour, salt, pepper, and milk. Cook three minutes or until smooth.

Put the potatoes and fish in a baking dish. Pour over the milk sauce, and cover with the buttered crumbs. Bake one-half hour in a moderately hot oven.

Salt Fish Balls

1 1/2 cups salt fish
1 egg or favorite substitute
3 cups potato
1/8 teaspoon pepper
2 tablespoons milk or favorite substitute
Cooking oil

Wash the fish, remove bones and cut into small pieces (scissors are best to use in cutting fish). Wash and pare the potatoes and cut in quarters. Put potatoes and fish in a stew pan and cover with boiling water. Boil until the potatoes are soft, twenty to twenty-five minutes. Turn into a colander and drain off all the water; return to the kettle and mash and beat until light. Add the milk, pepper, and egg well beaten. Shape in a large spoon, with a spatula. Fry in smoking-hot oil one minute. Drain on soft paper.

Fish Balls Made of Cooked Fish

Use the same proportions as given for Salt Fish Balls, using cooked fish which has been left over or canned fish, Salmon, or Tuna fish are good.

SOUPS AND CHOWDERS

CHAPTER VI

SOUPS AND CHOWDERS

CREAM OF POTATO SOUP

3 medium potatoes
4 cups milk or favorite substitute
1 onion
2 tablespoons butter or favorite substitute
1 teaspoon celery salt
1/2 teaspoon pepper
1 teaspoon salt
1 tablespoon flour

Wash and pare the potatoes; boil and rub through fine strainer. Put milk and onion (minced fine) on to cook in double boiler while potatoes are cooking. Melt the butter. Blend with it the flour and seasonings and stir into the hot milk. Cook five minutes. Pour slowly over the potatoes, stirring all the time. Boil up once and serve. One beaten egg added just before serving but not cooked in it improves it.

Potato and Onion Soup

3 medium potatoes
3 onions
3 small carrots
3 outside stalks of celery
1/2 cup celery sliced thin
1 slice bread
1/2 cup strained tomato

Wash, pare, and slice the potatoes, onions, and carrots. Wash and cut the celery stalks in inch pieces. Toast the bread hard and brown, and spread thickly with butter. Put all the above into a kettle. Add two quarts boiling water. Simmer for two or three hours. Rub through a sieve. Add the sliced celery and strained tomato, one teaspoon salt, and one-fourth teaspoon pepper. Cook for ten minutes and serve.

Purée of Vegetables

4 potatoes
2 small carrots
3 onions
4 tablespoons oil
sprig of parsley
1 teaspoon sugar
1 1/2 teaspoons flour
1 teaspoon salt
1 small turnip
½ teaspoon pepper

Cut all the vegetables into small pieces. Melt the fat. Add the onions, carrots, and parsley. Cook for five minutes but do not brown. Stir in the flour. Add potato and turnip, two quarts of boiling water, salt, pepper, and sugar. Boil for forty-five minutes. Rub through a fine strainer. If needed add more salt and pepper.

POTATO CHOWDER

4 large potatoes
1 tablespoon minced parsley
1 onion - chopped
1/2 teaspoon salt
2-inch cube salt pork
1/4 teaspoon pepper
2 cups boiling water
1 tablespoon butter or favorite substitute
2 cups milk or favorite substitute
1 1/2 tablespoons flour

Put the pork through meat chopper. Chop the onion. Wash, pare, and cut potatoes into dice. Fry the pork. Add the onion and cook until light brown. Add potatoes, parsley, salt, pepper, and water. Simmer until potatoes are soft. Make a sauce of the butter, flour, and milk, and add to the first mixture. Cook for five minutes. Add more salt and pepper if needed. Serve with crisp crackers.

FISH CHOWDER

1 pound fish
1 tablespoon salt pork cut or 1 tablespoon oil
4 potatoes in small pieces; or
1 onion
1 cup fish stock
1 cup hot milk or favorite substitute
2 tablespoons rice or corn flour
1 teaspoon salt
1/2 teaspoon pepper

Remove skin and bones from fish. Cover the skin and bones with cold water and put to cook. Simmer for ten or fifteen minutes. Pare and cut potatoes into dice. Mince the onion. Fry the pork. Remove the scraps. Add the onion and cook two or three minutes but do not brown. Add the flour. Drain water from bones and if there is not a cupful add enough hot water to fill the cup. Add to the onion and flour. Add the potato and fish cut into 1-inch pieces. Simmer until potatoes are soft. Add the hot milk, salt, and pepper. Put two crackers broken into quarters in the serving dish. Pour the chowder over them and serve. Sprinkle the pork scraps over the top. Strained tomato may be used in place of the milk.

Clam Chowder

4 cups sliced raw potato
1 onion - sliced
2 cups clams
1 teaspoon salt
1/2 cup salt pork cut into dice
1/4 teaspoon pepper
1 tablespoon flour
2 cups hot milk or favorite substitute
4 crackers

Fry the pork. Remove the scraps. Add the onion. Fry until a light brown. Add the flour. Put in layers of potatoes and clams. Cover with boiling water. Cook until the potatoes are soft (about fifteen minutes). Add the milk and four crackers broken into bits. Add more salt and pepper if needed. Oyster chowder may be made in the same manner.

Shrimp Chowder

1 cup diced cold boiled potatoes
1 tablespoon chopped onion
1 1/2 cups milk or favorite substitute
2 tablespoons minced salt pork or butter
1/2 cup cooked shrimps - chopped
1 tablespoon flour
salt and pepper

Fry the pork, or if butter is used, melt it, and cook the onion in it for a few moments, but do not brown. Add the flour and the milk.

Stir until smooth. Add the potato and shrimp and salt and pepper to taste. Simmer for five or six minutes. Serve with crisp crackers.

SALADS

CHAPTER VII

POTATO SALAD

Cold boiled potatoes cut in dice. Add one or two pimentos chopped fine, and a few drops of onion juice. Season with salt and pepper. For two cups of potato add two tablespoons oil and one tablespoon vinegar. In place of the pimentos two or three cold boiled beets may be used and one tablespoon chopped chives may be used in place of onion juice.

Russian Salad

1 cup cold cooked potato - diced
1/2 teaspoon salt
1 hard-boiled egg
1 cup cold cooked carrot - diced
6 shrimps - chopped
1 tablespoon chopped parsley
1/2 cup cold cooked peas
1 1/2 tablespoons vinegar
3 tablespoons oil
1/4 teaspoon paprika
Lettuce
mayonnaise

Mix the potato, carrot, and peas lightly with the oil, vinegar, salt, and paprika. Arrange on a bed of lettuce leaves. Mix four tablespoons mayonnaise with the parsley and shrimp and spread it on the salad. Garnish with the egg cut in slices.

Hungarian Potato Salad

2 cups cooked potato - sliced
1 small onion - minced fine
1 pickled beet cut in dice
1 smoked herring cut into small pieces
1 pickle - minced
2 tablespoons minced boiled ham
4 sardines - cut into small pieces

Mix lightly with four tablespoons oil, one and one-half tablespoons vinegar and one-half teaspoon paprika. Add salt if needed.

SERBIAN SALAD

4 cold boiled potatoes - diced
2 or 3 tablespoons cooked string beans
2 or 3 tablespoons cooked peas
2 tablespoons celery - minced
1/2 cucumber - diced
1 small onion - minced fine
2 tomatoes - diced
Watercress

Mix well with any good dressing, and serve on a bed of water cress.

HERRING SALAD (1)

1 cup mashed potato
2 small apples chopped
1/2 cup cold cooked meat chopped fine
1 cooked beet chopped
1 small onion minced fine
1 small dry herring soaked overnight, boned and chopped

Mix together. Add one-fourth teaspoon pepper, two tablespoons vinegar, and four tablespoons sour cream.

Herring Salad (2)

2 Holland herring, soaked overnight, boned, and cut in small pieces
4 medium boiled potatoes cut in thin slices
1 sour apple pared, cored, and sliced thin
2 hard-boiled eggs sliced

Toss up with French dressing and a little thick sour cream.

Spanish Onion Stuffed with Potato Salad

Peel the onions. Cut a slice from the top and remove all but the two outside layers. Chop the part removed with double the amount of cold boiled potato. Mix with French dressing. Fill the onions with this mixture and garnish with olives stuffed with pimentos, cut in halves lengthwise.

Potato Salad Dressing

1 medium potato boiled and mashed yolk of cooked egg
4 tablespoons oil
2 tablespoons vinegar
1 teaspoon mustard
1 teaspoon salt
cayenne

When potato is cold add the egg yolk, mustard, salt, and a few grains of cayenne. Add the oil, a little at a time, beating constantly, and lastly the vinegar slowly.

BOILED SALAD DRESSING

yolks of 2 eggs or favorite substitute
1/2 teaspoon mustard
1 teaspoon salt
Cayenne to taste
1/3 cup hot vinegar
2 tablespoons corn oil
1/2 cup sour cream

Beat the yolks slightly, add the seasonings, oil, and vinegar. Cook over water until it thickens, stirring constantly. When cool, add the cream and beat. Sweet cream may be used in place of sour if preferred.

God Bless Potatoes: Potato Cookery

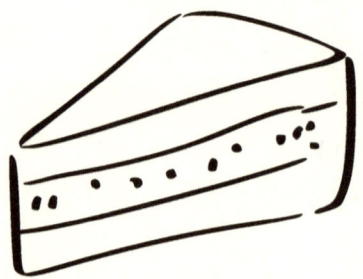

PUDDINGS AND CAKES

CHAPTER VIII

POTATO PUDDING

1 cup grated cold potato
2 cups milk or favorite substitute
3 eggs beaten lightly or favorite substitute
4 tablespoons sugar
1/4 teaspoon salt
1 tablespoon lemon juice
1 tablespoon melted butter or favorite substitute

Mix all the ingredients together. Pour into a well buttered baking dish and bake for half an hour.

Potato and Carrot Pudding

1 cup grated raw potato
¼ teaspoon mace
1 cup grated raw carrot
1 cup barley flour
1 cup seeded raisins
1/3 cup corn flour
1 cup butter
1/2 cup molasses
1 teaspoon cinnamon
1 teaspoon soda
1/4 teaspoon cloves

Steam three hours.

Minute Pudding

1/2 cup potato flour
2 eggs
1/8 teaspoon salt
1/2 cup corn syrup
4 cups milk
1/8 teaspoon salt

Heat three cups of milk in double boiler. Mix the flour and salt with the other cup of milk and stir into the hot milk. Stir until it thickens, then cook for ten minutes. Beat the eggs slightly; add the corn syrup and stir into the hot mixture. - Cook for five minutes stirring all the time. Pour into a serving dish and serve either hot or cold with cream and sugar.

Potato Fruit Pudding

1 cup mashed potato
2 tablespoons baking powder
1 1/2 tablespoons butter or favorite substitute
2 cups rice flour
1/4 teaspoon ginger or cinnamon
1/2 teaspoon salt
1 egg milk or favorite substitute
fruit of your choice

Sift flour, baking powder, salt, and spice together. Add the butter, using the tips of fingers to mix with. Add the potato and egg beaten light, and enough milk to make a soft dough. Put the fruit, which may be cherries, blackberries, blueberries, or sliced peaches into a baking dish. Add enough sugar or corn syrup to sweeten. Cover with the dough and cut slashes in top to allow steam to escape. Either bake for half an hour or steam for one hour. Serve with a sweet sauce.

Orange Dumplings

1 cup cold mashed potato
1/4 teaspoon ginger
1 cup corn flour
1 egg or favorite substitute
1 cup wheat flour
3 teaspoons baking powder
2 tablespoons butter or favorite substitute
Milk or favorite substitute
oranges

Sift the baking powder, ginger, and corn and wheat flour together. Add the potato, butter, and egg beaten light, and enough milk to make a stiff dough. Turn onto a floured board and roll to half an inch thick. Cut into three-inch squares and lay pieces of orange on each square. Sprinkle with sugar and draw the corners over the orange. Steam for one hour or bake for thirty-five minutes. Serve with:

Orange Sauce

Mix one tablespoon arrowroot with a little cold water. Add one cup boiling water and boil for five minutes. Add the juice of one orange and the grated rind of half an orange, one teaspoon lemon juice, and one-half cup sugar. Cook for five minutes. Add one tablespoon of butter, and serve. Cornstarch may be used in place of arrowroot, but must be cooked ten to fifteen minutes.

Fruit Sauce

1/2 cup sugar
1 tablespoon butter or favorite substitute
1/2 cup canned or fresh fruit or jelly
1 cup boiling water
2 tablespoons cornstarch
1 tablespoon lemon juice

If an acid jelly is used the lemon juice may be omitted. Mix cornstarch with the sugar. Add the boiling water and cook for ten minutes. Add the fruit or jelly. If canned or fresh fruit is used put through a strainer.

Short Cake

1 cup hot mashed potato
4 teaspoons baking powder
1 cup corn flour
1/2 teaspoon salt
1/2 cup milk or favorite substitute
4 tablespoons butter or favorite substitute
1 tablespoon sugar

Boil one large or two medium potatoes. When soft rub through a fine wire strainer. Measure one cupful and add the milk. Sift together the corn flour, salt, sugar, and baking powder. Rub in the butter with the tips of the fingers. Add the potato and put into a well greased shallow baking tin. Smooth it over the top with a spatula until the pan is covered and the top smooth. Bake for half an hour in a moderately hot oven. When done split with a heated knife and spread with butter and cover with mashed and sweetened berries or peaches.

Sponge Cake

3/4 cup sugar
1/4 teaspoon salt
1/2 cup potato flour
2 eggs or favorite substitute
1 teaspoon baking powder
4 tablespoons cold water
1 teaspoon lemon juice

Beat the yolks, sugar, water, and lemon juice together until thick and light. Sift the flour twice, then once with the baking powder and salt. Mix lightly with the first mixture. Fold in the whites beaten stiff and light. Bake twenty-five to thirty minutes in a moderate oven.

CHOCOLATE CAKE

2 eggs or favorite substitute
1/3 cup sugar
2 tablespoons butter
1 square bakers' chocolate
2 tablespoons corn syrup
1/2 teaspoon vanilla
1/2 cup potato flour
1 teaspoon baking powder
salt to taste

Melt the chocolate over water. Add the syrup, butter, and milk. Beat the eggs and sugar together until light. Add the salt and vanilla, and combine the two mixtures. Beat well. Add the flour and baking powder. Pour into well buttered small cake tins. Bake fifteen to twenty minutes. This rule will make a dozen small cakes.

SCOTCH DROP CAKES

1/2 cup mashed potato
1/4 cup honey
1/2 cup oatmeal -finely ground
1/4 cup butter or favorite substitute
1 egg or favorite substitute
1/2 cup rye flour
1/2 teaspoon soda
milk

Mix all the ingredients together except milk. Then add enough milk to make just stiff enough to drop from a spoon. Drop by spoonfuls on a buttered sheet and bake in a moderately hot oven ten to fifteen minutes.

CHOCOLATE NOUGAT CAKE

1/2 cup potato
1/2 cup grated chocolate
1/2 cup butter
1/2 cup almonds- chopped
1/2 cup sugar
1/2 cup corn syrup
2 eggs or favorite substitute
1/4 cup milk or favorite substitute
2 teaspoons baking powder
1 1/8 cups barley flour
a few grains of salt

Either grate or rub through a wire strainer enough cold cooked potato to make half a cupful. Cream the butter; add sugar, corn syrup, and the beaten yolks of eggs. Beat well. Add the potato. Sift salt and baking powder with the flour and add with the chocolate, nuts, and milk to the first mixture. Beat the whites of eggs until light and stiff and fold in lightly. Bake in a buttered cake tin, forty minutes in a moderate oven. Other nuts may be used if preferred.

Potato Doughnuts

3 potatoes
1/2 cup barley flour
2 tablespoons butter
4 tablespoons corn syrup
1/4 cup sugar
1/4 teaspoon nutmeg
2 eggs or favorite substitute
1/4 teaspoon baking soda
1/2 cup sour milk or buttermilk or favorite substitute
1 teaspoon baking powder
wheat flour

Boil and mash the potatoes. Add the butter, sugar, corn syrup, and nutmeg. Beat the eggs light and add them with the milk. Sift the soda, baking powder, and barley flour together. Add enough wheat flour to make a soft dough. Flour the board. Pat to half an inch thickness; cut out and fry in deep fat.

INDEX

A Complete Meal........................51
Baked Ham and Potatoes..............55
Baked Hash Brown Potatoes..........17
Baked Potatoes............................16
Baked Sweet Potatoes..................47
Boiled Potatoes............................15
Boiled Salad Dressing................71
Boiled Sweet Potatoes..............47
Browned Sweet Potatoes...............48
Cheese Sauce..............................28
Chilian Potatoes..........................35
Chocolate Cake...........................79
Chocolate Nougat Cake...............80
Clam Chowder............................65
Colcannon...................................22
Cottage Pie.................................52
Cream of Potato Soup..................61
Curried Potatoes.........................19
Delmonico Potatoes....................23
Fish a la Murphy.........................57
Fish an Potato Scallop.................58
Fish Balls made with Cooked Fish..59
Fish Chowder..............................64
Franconia Potatoes......................24
French Potatoes...........................35
Fried Sweet Potatoes...................48
Fruit Sauce..................................77
Giblet Stew.................................52
Glazed Sweet Potatoes................48
Hashed Brown Potatoes...............17
Herring Salad 1...........................69
Herring Salad 2...........................70
Hollandaise Sauce 31
Hungarian Potato Salad...............68

Kalecannon........................22
Kentucky Potatoes..............32
Liver en Casserole 54
Mashed Potatoes.......................15
Minute Pudding........................74
Norwegian Potatoes...................33
Orange Dumplings....................76
Orange Sauce...........................76
Pepper Pot................................53
Philadelphia Potatoes................32
Potatoes and Onions..................23
Potato and Carrot Pudding 7   4
Potato and Corn Muffins............41
Potato and Nut Croquettes.........36
Potato and Nut Croquettes 2......37
Potato and Onion Soup.............62
Potato and Spinach Croquettes..36
Potato Balls..............................27
Potato Biscuit 1........................40
Potato Biscuit 2........................41
Potato Bouchées.......................26
Potato Cakes............................28
Potato Casserole.......................55
Potato Cheese Soufflé...............29
Potato Chops...........................25
Potato Chowder.......................63
Potato Croustades....................56
Potato Doughnuts....................81
Potato Dumplings 1.................45
Potato Dumplings 2.................46
Potato Fricassee.......................20
Potato Fruit Pudding................75
Potato Gruyére........................30
Potato Hillocks........................21

Potato Nests with Cheese............29
Potato Noodles........................44
Potato Omelette......................22
Potato Pancakes 1..................44
Potato Pancakes 2..................45
Potato Pie.................................24
Potato Pudding.......................73
Potato Puffs............................18
Potato Quenelles....................46
Potato Roll...............................31
Potato Salad...........................67
Potato Salad Dressing.............70
Potato Sauté............................16
Potato Scallop........................20
Potato Scones.........................42
Potato Soufflé.........................19
Potato, Rye, and Oatmeal Muffins............................42
Potatoes a la Maitre d'Hotel.....16
Potatoes and Sausage...............54
Potatoes Hashed in Cream........18
Potatoes Mexican Style........35
Potatoes with Cheese Stuffing....30
Potatoes with Chives.................21
Purée of Vegetables...............62
Raised Potato Biscuit.............39
Russian Salad........................68
Salt Fish Balls.......................59
Savory Liver............................53
Scalloped Herring....................57
Scotch Bannocks....................43
Scotch Drop Cakes.................79
Scotch Potatoes.......................34
Serbian Salad..........................69
Short Cake..............................77
Shrimp Chowder.....................65
Spanish Onion Stuffed with Potato Salad................................70

Sponge Cake................................78
Stuffing for Roast Goose 2................57
Stuffing for Roast Goose or Duck....56
Sweet Potato Croquettes................49
Sweet Potatoes with Apples...........48
Sweet Potatoes with Orange...........49
Swiss Potatoes..............................34
Tomato Sauce..............................27

Other restored and reprinted cookbooks
from NYHR

The Modernized International Jewish Cook Book
by Florence Kreisler Greenbaum, 1919

German Cookery for the American Home
by Ella Oswald, 1910

*The Art of German Cooking and Baking
Recipes to Keep Your Heritage Alive*
by Lina Meier, 1922

*The Pilgrim Cookbook: Recipes
from German Church Ladies*
1921

Visit us on the web

www.NewCenturyGermanCooking.com

and join our "German Cooking" group on Facebook

www.ingramcontent.com/pod-product-compliance
Lightning Source LLC
LaVergne TN
LVHW011429080426
835512LV00005B/339